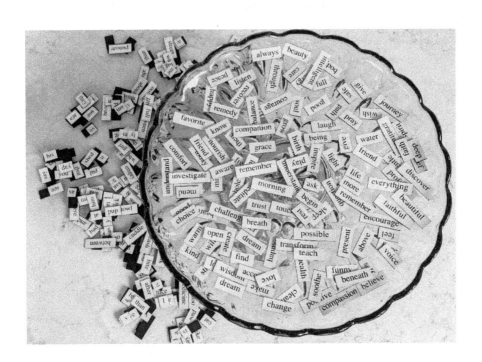

Magnetic Poems

Dawn Anderson, CreatetheDawn

OTHER WORK BY DAWN

For more of Dawn's positive poetry & journaling, read:

- *Seeing the Beauty in Everyday Things*
- Nature Series of chapter books
- *Change Your Life Journal*, a guided journal
- *Tiny Poems*
- *I am the Boss of my Bears*. An emotion management book for children (and adults)
- three Stamp-Poem books
    - *Stamp Collection*
    - *Stamp Collection II*
    - *World Stamp-Poems*

Search: **amazon.com/author/createthedawn**

Or, visit her blog, *CreatetheDawn* at:
www.createthedawn.com

Copyright © 2023 Dawn Anderson, CreatetheDawn

All rights reserved.

ISBN: **9798397055406**

Cover and closing photos by Dawn Anderson.
Author's Note photo cropped from a photo by Robert Mentzer taken at my inauguration as the first Wausau Poet Laureate.

DEDICATION

To holiday dinner guests
– family, friends, and added guests without family nearby.

Magnetic Poems

CONTENTS

	Introduction	ix
1	Feel Grace	Pg. 1
2	Deep Wish	Pg. 3
3	Positive Beauty	Pg. 4
4	Give Possible	Pg. 5
5	More Soul	Pg. 6
6	Accept Journey	Pg. 7
7	Inner Joy	Pg. 8
8	Weight Wisdom	Pg. 9
9	Nourish Believe	Pg. 10
10	Laugh Through	Pg. 11
11	Free Spirit	Pg. 12
12	Sooth Aware	Pg. 13
13	Heal Mind	Pg. 14
14	Safe Truth	Pg. 15
15	Mend Pray	Pg. 16
16	Warm Peace	Pg. 17
17	Voice Relief	Pg. 18
18	Breath Touch	Pg. 19
19	Whole Trust	Pg. 20

20	Body Faith	Pg. 21
21	Birth Path	Pg. 22
22	Listen Life	Pg. 23
23	Live Light	Pg. 24
24	Hard Gift	Pg. 25
25	Better Balance	Pg. 26
26	Dream Remedy	Pg. 27
27	Being Rest	Pg. 28
28	Friend Heart	Pg. 29
29	Begin Cycle	Pg. 30
30	Grow Full	Pg. 31
31	Say Gentle	Pg. 32
32	Create Love	Pg. 34
33	Recover Gratitude	Pg. 35
34	Transform Comfort	Pg. 36
35	Present Profound	Pg. 37
36	Courage Medicine	Pg. 38
37	Encourage Today	Pg. 39
38	Always Remember	Pg. 40
39	Will Hope	Pg. 41
	Author's Note	Pg. 42

ACKNOWLEDGMENTS

Gratefulness to write in a language with so many words and nuances - English. A language that welcomes words from other languages as well as new made-up words. A language that has evolved and grown through history documenting the old while adapting to current culture and events.

These poems explore meaning in pairs of words. Acknowledging how powerful and versatile just two words can be.

Dawn Anderson

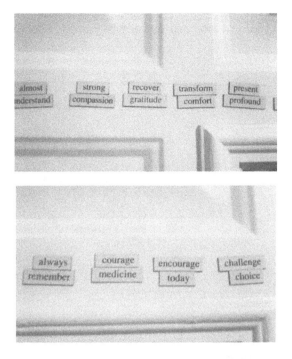

INTRODUCTION

Remember when magnetic words were a thing? I had two sets, not on my refrigerator, on the front door. One thanksgiving, my magnetic words were secretly paired by dinner guests. The paired words took on deep meanings after walking past the door many times. I snapped photos of them thinking someday they would become poems.

Twenty years later, on the 20th anniversary of National/Global Poetry Writing Month, they finally birthed poems.

Feel free to borrow any of the word parings for your own poems. Enjoy this collection of positive, intelligent poems. -Dawn

1 FEEL GRACE

Here we go, our first word pairing prompt poem. How do you "feel grace"?

Feel Grace

That holy place inside
Inner temple
Church of the soul
Blue sky inward
Star light pure night
Breathed in
through pores
and portals
Heart
Crown
Root
Upheld palms
and feet in green pastures.

Really   feel   grace

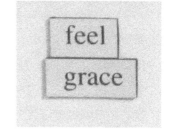

2 DEEP WISH

Oh, this is fun. Exploring how deep these old magnetic word pairings go. This one went to the underworld through a wishing well.

Enjoy the poem and your own journey into the deep.

Deep Wish

Wishing well
Mercury gray
Pebble rippled
Deep
Below water table
Water sign
Fluid as life

Deep wish
Given to the underworld
Niflheim
Not where evil dwells
where we do our shadow work,
we shed old skins
baptized again
in primal waters
to immerge washed
A new day

3 POSITIVE BEAUTY

We're into the swing of it now. This word pairing prompt was a curious one. I wondered what meaning it would produce. Being 54 years old, my idea of a person's beauty is changing, enriching. Enjoy the poem and let your positive beauty shine out.

Positive Beauty

Flowing locks
thin.
Flawless skin
mars.
Tall spine
compacts.

Smile
never fades.
Hug
Warms.
Wisdom
shares.
Patience
grows.
Joy
flows.

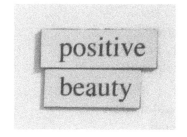

4 GIVE POSSIBLE

Our next word pairing is "give possible." It is probably true how matrixed we are in our small world. There is a "Six Handshake Rule" that we are socially connected within six "degrees." So, why not give each other possibilities in this wild wonderful world we share. Enjoy the poem!

Give Possible

Possibility thinker
Sharer
Maker
Giver
Yes
Uplift others
Gift of imagination
Inspiration
Hutzpah
Yes sah -
If no man is an island
then we are interconnected
Mycelium
Finger tips touching
Wonder twin powers
connect
Give the possible
and it will circle 'round to you.

5 MORE SOUL

Interesting word pairing for our prompt. Two poems started forming in my mind. One meaning of Soul is the spiritual one. The other, funk soul and soul food. I loved the Southern cooking at Papa's Soul Food Kitchen in Eugene, Oregon until Papa died and the restaurant closed. Here's to Papa for both meanings of the word Soul. Enjoy the poem and some BBQed pork ribs.

More Soul

Depth
Rhythm
Groove thang
Hips gyrate
Lungs inflate
Never irate
Suave and
Smooooth

More soul
Depth of character
Rhythm of life
Groove and move
Healthy body
Healthy soul
Happy soul
Spreading love
Infectious love
More soul
Mo betta

6 ACCEPT JOURNEY

Our 6th word pairing prompt. So often our need for control is what causes us stress, is what causes us to miss the good in the hard. A journey is not a plan, it is discovery while headed in a general direction. Ponder the poem.

Accept Journey

Uniquely ours,
our journey
Half free will
Half fate and genetics
Serenity prayer
Journey of dreams
Journey of doors
opening and closing
stand tall
lean into
the possible
around the potholes
for they are part of the road
for they are what makes us.

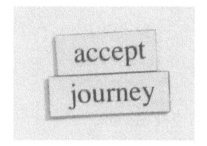

"Go gcoinní Dia i mbos A láimhe thú"
"May the road rise up to meet you.
May the wind be always on your back"

7 INNER JOY

Our 7th word pairing is a fun one. Laugh my friends, laugh. Most days, joy is a choice and can be created with simple pleasures. The Hank Crawford album I reference is *Wildflower* from 1973. The *Hart to Hart* reference is a vintage television series about a happily in-love detective couple. Enjoy the poem.

Inner Joy

Genuine joy
lives in the blood
spills out in love puddles
of mirth and giggles,
funny bone essentials.
Crank your Hank Crawford
wuh kuh wuh kuh
inner butterflies dance
while eyes see the good
and the good with attention
grows and spreads.
Contagion is joy
go forth and infest
pandemic of joy
heart to heart
and Hart to Hart.

8 WEIGHT WISDOM

This one took a bit of noodling to find its meaning. Looking up definitions and synonyms helps me see a key word from many angles. It jump-starts the poem and the writing then finds its way. The "wisdom" synonym "prudence" hit a Beatles inspired path for this poem. Find your meaning.

Weight Wisdom

Burden of wisdom?
Density of wisdom?
Gravity, Pressure, substance?
Caution of wisdom?
Dear Prudence*
come out to play.
Wisdom is our sanity
and insanity
for the more we know
the more we want to know.
Dear Prudence
it's a sunny day
look 'round
for all is one
even if not evenly weighted.
Weight of knowing
the all-knowing within.
Dear Prudence

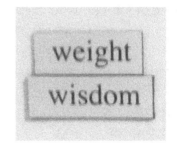

9 NOURISH BELIEVE

This magical poem came out of a weekend with kids; seeing the world through their fresh eyes. Yes, we played Mad Libs. Conjure up some magic for your world.

Nourish Believe

A healthy belief in magic
promises a sparkly heart.
Like Mad Lib lines
let chance surprise you.
Little happenings delight like
a leaf landing in your path,
coupon for chocolate
on the back of the City Pages,
thinking of a friend who calls the next day.

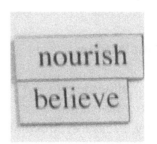

Believe in good for you see what you believe.
Circumstance and happenstance
wonder do make.
Wonder the key to escaping chains of judgment.
Always choices
Always chances.
Nourish belief in magic
to not miss the precious.

10 LAUGH THROUGH

Daily happenings often inform a poem. We really did have a funeral today noticing the laughing at the photo board, in speeches, between tears, and during the meal after closure. "Gone but not forgotten" is "Laugh Through."

Laugh Through

Funeral today.
What I love about funerals
they are not all sadness and crying.
There is remembering
and stories
and laughing.

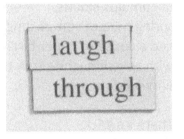

We hold up this person
in gratitude,
forgiveness,
and love.
In our hearts,
we hold the laughter shared with them.

With each passing friend
our heart fills.
Feeling warmth
even through loss.

11 FREE SPIRIT

Day 11's word pairing prompt is perfect for me. Friends will smile when they read this poem. Enjoy!

Free Spirit

Mom said
to not let anyone
squash my spirit.
A spirit that hovers
between the fat bottoms
of cumulus clouds,
spring mud of composting leaves,
and a copse of paper birch
with two slim white tree trunks
entwined.

There's a trick
the song birds use
flapping their wings
to lift their colorful bodies.
Between beats
they sink
then press the air again
boosted upward.

Spirit is like this.

12 SOOTH AWARE

This word pairing drew out an intense poem for those of us with high intuition, connector personalities, sometimes called "Empaths." What works best to protect myself is to rock, read, write, rest. My soothing sanctuary is an off-grid 140-year-old fieldstone homestead with a woodstove and a rocking chair. Find your sanctuary.

Sooth Aware   for Empaths.

Our feelers reach out
like the roots of an Aspen tree
reading faces
absorbing energy around us
intuition radiant
we connect
we love
we heal others.

Our compassionate hearts ping
and ping and ping.
Weight of empathy
can overwhelm.

Sooth awareness
with breath, sleep, routine,
connecting to our own mood.
Find sanctuary
from the swirling seas
the school of fish.

The world needs us
but not today.
Not Saturday.
That is our day.
Me day

13 HEAL MIND

I wrote this silly poem in one of those slap happy moods your mind goes to protecting itself from stressing. We were watching old *Seinfeld* episodes and laughing while I scribbled down this little gem. Enjoy the poem.

Heal Mind

Mind meld
Mr. Spock
A logical mind
is a shame to waste.
Heal our brains
with fatty fish
and avocado.
Mind over matter
Does that really matter?
Protons matter to mass
Mass on Sunday
but it's the electrons that spin
and the planet spins
The mind reels/reals
The mind heals.

14 SAFE TRUTH

Day 14 word pairing prompt. Eeks this one got a little preachy and advicey. After yesterday's healed mind poem, this poem must be a way to keep our mind healthy. Like we said in the "Nourish Believe" poem day 9, "you see what you believe."

Safe Truth

Safe truth is our own truth
not one spun to sell
clickbait money maker.
Safe truth we see with our values
spun "truth" plays our emotions.
Relate safe truth to its real size
mountain or molehill.
In the grand scheme perspective
attention to our small sphere of control,
attention to our molehill.
Safe truth is inside my door
and on my door step
where I sweep first.

15 MEND PRAY

This 15th word pairing brought to mind that childhood prayer "now I lay me down to sleep."
Of course, our own efforts and choices direct our lives, but there is power in affirmations, intention setting, visioning, and especially gratefulness. Prayer and meditation tap into that power. And, as did that childhood prayer, it's a way to acknowledge and accept death and the things we cannot control. Here is my modernized version of the prayer.

Mend Pray

Bring back nightly prayer
to God, Universe, the Great Bear.

"I rest in your unending love"
please bless the earth and sky above.
"May the angels watch me through the night"
and gird my innate kindness, sense, and might.
"I pray the Lord my soul to keep"
for my hopes and dreams run deep
but "if I die before I wake"
I am grateful for the memories I will take.

16 WARM PEACE

Warm peace because, well, I guess there cannot be a fight for peace. We can fight for freedom but not peace directly. "Believe, see, find, create" peace in your life. Hug.

Warm Peace

Warm peace
A peaceful peace
We cannot force peace
We believe, see, find, create
Peace
in ourselves
in our homes
Peace is more powerful
than force
It begins with forgiveness
Faith in good

17 VOICE RELIEF

I wrote this poem to our word pairing amidst the sound clutter of an airport. We need those healing silent times where talking is out of place; when we can be present to nature around us. Enjoy the poem.

Voice Relief

Quiet the electric chatter
Silence of nature's voice
Wind that rolls across treetops
moving the clouds
yet unruffled are the purple coneflowers
and bright-eyed daisies.
Creak of age-dried rocking chair
Purr of curled lap cat
No need for words
human constructs
mumblings.
Breath the true voice
Eyes true communication.

18 BREATH TOUCH

This word pairing prompt recalled the loss of breath touch during COVID19. Especially in the beginning of the pandemic, closeness took on a fearful tint. Some of that surely lingers. This poem is in celebration of the ebb of that fear.

Breath Touch

Past our breath fears
Intimacy of shared spaces
Energy exchange
Eyes windows to emotions
Touch of a friend's breath
in laughter and whispered stories.

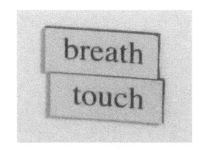

Tell me a secret
close, in my eager ear.

Kiss me on the lips
deep as cavernous love.

Hold my hand
stroking that delicate spot
with your fingertips.

Brush your cheek against mine
sigh into a hug,
heart beating to beating heart.

Whisper sweet words
vulnerable sentiments
I love you!

19 WHOLE TRUST

In case you missed how these word pairing prompts came to be...I had two sets of magnetic words on my front door. Dinner quests arranged them into pairs. I took photos and 20 years later am finally using them to inspire poems for Global/National Poetry Writing month.

This pairing was powerful and a little uncomfortable to explore. Trust certainly does start with my confidence before the trustworthiness of the other. Explore with me.

Whole Trust

Not the cat kind
with one eye cracked
Not "trust but verify"
Not snoop just to be sure
but whole trust
my heart in your hands
Requires trust in myself
Brave enough to know
to not worry or wonder
A trust to settle into
to lie back supported
a foundation.

20 BODY FAITH

This was a fun one. Our bodies are amazing healing creatures. In my fifth decade inhabiting this vessel, a rosehip metaphor came up. Rosehips come after bloom and propagate new plants.

Body Faith

I am not delicate
A flower, maybe not in bloom,
a rosehip
strong
making seed for future generations.

Faith in my body
my castle
Daily stretches
Morning breaths
Breaking adhesions
Expanding lungs
Expanding mind
Garden food
Supple veins
Busy hands
Joyful thoughts.

21 BIRTH PATH

Right away this word pairing prompt had to be an ancestor poem. How and who we came to be is a stumbling of 400 generations. This ripple effect through humankind might be why we are so interested in ancestry and history. Ponder the poem.

Birth Path

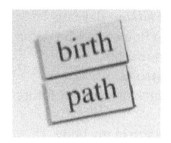

Trail of ancestors' lives
Travel months to henge
Dowry exchange
Mixture of genes
Hunter, Farmer, Craftsman
Smith, Shaman, Chieftain
War and conquer
Slave or victor
Escape famine
Escape persecution
Promise of dreams
Indenture to new world
Follow work
Chase land
Comfort or adventure
Chance and choices.
Each generation forages
the path
       given
              followed
                     created.

22 LISTEN LIFE

This word pairing is a good boost for me as I settle into comfortable routines. Enter the world of remote work. Anywhere with laptop and Wi-Fi is my office. A week working remotely from Florida not only was less stressful, it gave me the time and hutzpah to tackle and complete some nagging work. Listen to life's nudges.

Listen Life

Life sends you nudges.
What treasure lies behind the next "yes"?
Listen deeply
Pushing doubt and routine aside
"'The long and winding 'road' less traveled'"
We are tourists here
See the sights
Learn and wonder
Seek, go, do.

23 LIVE LIGHT

A beautiful day at home playing "fantasy ambiance music" and watching the birds. Perfect day for "Live Light" prompt to come up. Day 23. Enjoy the poem and put some spring in your day.

Live Light

Light of mind
Flowing with dainty butterfly wings
Gentle my sway with the clouds

Light of body
Skipping in new attitude shoes
Twirling in my twirly dressed hips

Light of touch
like stroking a baby's cheek
I tiptoe on the delicate ground
Grounded am I.

Light of spirit
Flute tremolo
Seeing gnomes
with their nature gifts
Breathing in the fluff of each day

Live light
Live joy

24 HARD GIFT

I knew this poem needed to be about letting go and trusting loved ones to make their own way in the world. My first attempt came out preachy and boring. This second attempt is a cliché metaphor but the last two lines made it good enough.

Hard Gift

Feathers have grown
pins to plumes
Bulbous bird bodies
nestled in the shrinking nest

Fledge baby birds
Fledge
Fly be free
in the wild blue
Take to the air
with mother's trust
though the shadows of hawks
like ghostly banshees
skim open spaces

To fly with chance
is better than caged in safety.

25 BETTER BALANCE

I wrote a poem "Turning to Stone" about the stiffening and creepingly increasing discomfort in the body as we age. This month, my sister introduced me to the MELT Method - Myofascial Energetic Length Technique. Perfect timing as my Spring equinox mantras are: I am a creature of love, I am a creator, I am supple and strong. That last mantra was to combat turning to stone. This poem explores that balance of the body in aging.

Better Balance

Tippy canoe
Bailing water
coming in fast
Breath like a rocky stream
Trickle and bubble

MELT into the stream
Supple and flow
Align and balance
Softening stone
to molten fascia.

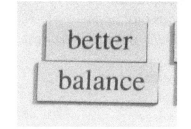

26 DREAM REMEDY

"Dream Remedy" is our magnetic word pairing today. Interesting combination as we encourage our dreams, not let them go. But, sometimes we hold onto a pipe dream too long instead of noticing the real possibilities all around us. Reassess your dreams.

Dream Remedy

Carrying that red balloon
Believing in a checklist
Skipping hope down the aisle.
There is a moon in my eye
coloring what I see.

How does a river plan?

Dream remedy is flow,
wonder, surprise.
My course ever changing,
eroding, evolving.
Blue pool to rest and ponder.
Waterfall to let go
into continuous flow.

27 BEING REST

Sleep has been a lifelong exploration and learning. Luckily, most nights, with good habits and practices, glorious rest is there waiting. Rest well my dears with this day 27 word pairing for poetry writing month.

Being Rest

Belly breath, long exhale
Nothing else to do but sleep
Mind drifts to sea
Bed a pea green boat.
Be rest
Heavy in clean cool sheets
Embracing darkness
the sleeping night.
Be rest
Fold into restoration
like butter in puff pastry
Tomorrow is another day
Nothing else to do but rest
Let go from head to toe
Rolling wave pushing out day's ills
Moon juice washing cells clean.

28 FRIEND HEART

I wrote this poem in the company of close girlfriends. You can feel the love oozing out. Cherish true friends. Day 28 Magnetic word pairing prompt.

Friend Heart

Generous
Round and lush
Puddles of love
Cup overflowing
Arms warm and generous
like grandma's cookies
oven gooey
full of sweet chocolate.
Heart of a friend
Open ears
Seeks to know your heart
to understand wishes, needs
Helping hands
Loving words
Friend heart

29 BEGIN CYCLE

A deep-thought inquiring poem came from this word pairings. What are some other blurry-edged cycle examples?

Begin Cycle

Does a cycle have a beginning and end?
or does it slip into the next loop
blurry and slow moving?
Snow on a spring Robin's tail
Hills and valleys of menopause
Death infiltrating life
Year into year
Umma, Lunisolar, Julian, Gregorian.
Ashes and dust both
the beginning and the end.
Maybe a cycle is returning,
a begin again.

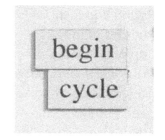

30 GROW FULL

For most of these word pairings prompts, the poems sparked instantly. This one took some chewing then quickly grew. Enjoy the poem and your food. Day 30 Magnetic word pairing.

Grow Full

A lesson in eating
Grow full
Slow fill
Slow food
Orange and green
pulled from dirt
Sensory chew and crunch
Taste of earth
Taste of health
Grow enjoy
Grow fulfilled.

31 SAY GENTLE

This word pairing seems a call for the return of emotion management where relationship is more precious than emotion of the moment. Bonus poem 31.

Say Gentle

Truth with soft edges
and warm eyes.
Say gentle your peace
when it will matter.
Quiet thy heavy tongue
when it does not serve.

32 CREATE LOVE

The best for last (as if there is ever a last). Let's create some love together. Thank you for following along with these magnetic word pairing poems for Global Poetry writing month. I have a few word pairings left, so please keep reading along.

Create Love

Create Love
out of sticks and stones
wrapped in colored yarn
and hung on the front door
like a Christmas wreath.
Always carry a Love kit
in a back pocket,
quick draw,
for moments of love.
Create Love from words,
deeds,
thoughtful thoughts,
even intentions.
The clay of love is all around,
the planet wheel spinning,
our hands dexterous
with imagination.
Look, look
at the moon and stars for patterns
to create
       great Love.

33 RECOVER GRATITUDE

We did 32 poems to these magnetic word pairings for the month. Well, there are seven left from my door 20 years ago when my Thanksgiving fairies arranged the pairings. I still do not know who put them together which makes them even more special. Here comes #33 and an intention to publish them all in a book for us. Oh, credit to my friend Ashley for coining a "pandemic of entitlement" for this poem.

Recover Gratitude

In this pandemic of entitlement
this time of "I deserve"
when every emotion is somehow sacred,
a right to geyser it out
without counting to 10
or finding kind words
following kindergarten wisdom
to consider the feelings of others.

The remedy
is rediscovering gratitude.
Scheduling joy
snack time, nap time,
breathe and journal,
walk in the woods,
listen to birdsong,
sing, dance, jump in puddles
kiss, hug, say "I love you,"
say "I love me,"
be,
be grateful,
reclaim childlike gratitude,
spread a pandemic of gratefulness.

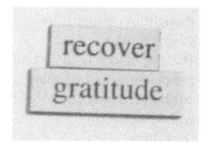

34 TRANSFORM COMFORT

At a summit last week with a room full of artists and all their lovely quirks, the meaning of this word pairing prompted poem was inspired. Reflecting on the interesting people I have had the pleasure to meet (and learn from) the growing list includes: Harley riders, witches, belly dancers, ex-cons, devout church goers, bird watchers, farmers, physicians, eastern medicine practitioners, psychics, poets, painters, coders, loggers, sports stars, wanderers, business executives, stay home moms, Mennonites, big rig truck drivers, butchers, bakers, candlestick makers, people from so many other counties/cultures, and….

Transform Comfort

Social comfort that is.
Bring wonder to a crowd.
Curiosity to meet
the strangest person in the room.
Shake a new hand.
Learn their story
What does the world look like
from their window?
Transform social comfort
with social adventure
Discover new landscapes, ideas,
new interests and new friends.
With wonder, venture
"Hello my name is Dawn,
I'd like to meet you."

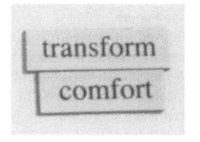

35 PRESENT PROFOUND

This word pairing poem took an ancient history and mystical turn. Research rabbit holes can lead to profound places. Synonyms of "profound" lead me to "hermetic" and to the ancient figure of Hermes Trismegistus and his attributed text the *Hermetica*. The *Hermetica* references 1st-3rd century spells and incantations. The invention of the hermetic seal is also attributed to Hermes Trismegistus from a time when science, astrology, and magic were interconnected.

Present Profound

Profound intention
spell poem
infused with wisdom and charm,
charm that loveliness and swagger.
A spell incast with enchanted words
incanted under moonlight with melodic voice
is present profound
bewitching
or maybe just provoking tenderness
that lives in us
like cradling a chick
or stroking a purring cat
it opens us
and sets the magic free
to reach out
whether to nearby flower
or a friend around the world,
therefore, a poem can be
a heart-door
opening to oneness,
a lovingkindness spell
through which we
present profound
for all who will hear.

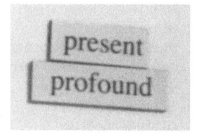

36 COURAGE MEDICINE

Rarely do I scrap poems. They seem to come out organically from somewhere, a muse or divine intervention. But, this one started with a concept with too many other possible, and not positive, meanings. So, I scrapped all but the last stanza and caulked cracks creating a new, short poem. What is your courage medicine to heal your core wound?

Courage Medicine

Courage medicine
the antidote to security fear
I'd say is peace, presence, trust.
Peace in plenty
Presence in now
Trust like a lioness
in my skills
my stealth and speed,
in my companions.

37 ALWAYS REMEMBER

While not planned, "Always Remember" word-pairing came up for Memorial Day. Writing a memorial poem is challenging to honor sacrifice, celebrate freedom yet not celebrate war. This two-page poem came spilling out at 2 a.m. in the private dark with tears in my eyes. Hopefully the poem speaks to you and honors war veterans.

Always Remember

Those who had no choice not to go
Those who got caught up in the promise of glory
Those who died
Those who lived
Those with affected bodies and minds.

Always remember
young frightened boy
against young frightened boy
separated only by uniform and country
into friend or foe.
The young people
fighting the wars of old men's power and greed.

Always remember
Those at home
the mothers
the fathers
the victory gardens

the rations
the worry and tears.
All that lies forgotten
are the reasons
if ever truly known.

Today
Memorial Day
remember in our small ways
to have no foe
to see past politics and flags
to see humanity
to see young boys and girls
mothers and fathers.
To always remember
the sacrifices of war.

38 ENCOURAGE TODAY

I love this little happy poem reminding us each day is a gift for which to be grateful. Have a wonderful day!

Encourage Today

Served on a platter
garnished with ease
of modern comforts.
I bring myself to this day
with the choices time awards
to "spend" it as carefully
as a last dollar.
To relish this day,
smell sweet spring air,
taste my abundance,
and suspend worry
for worry belongs to tomorrow
which may never come.

I stretch languidly
with the arc of sun
shining out what is everything,
no matter the number of my days,
Love.

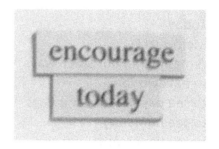

39 WILL HOPE

The last of the Magnetic word pairing prompted poems. The intelligence and wisdom that these paired words gave us needs to be brought together in this collection.

For this poem, it took three running starts depending upon the meaning of "will" either as a verb or noun. It was interesting to play with "will" as it adds action to "hope." Since action is probably the secret to getting what we hope for, this poem ended up pretty spot on. Enjoy the poem go for your hopes.

Will Hope

To will hope is action.
Magic is in the mundane.
Achieve the ends
by intention
and the means to get there.

I will hope
I will dream
I will take my own baby steps.
Hope fuels change
change of my choice.

I will hope
resilience and adaptation.
Movement of mind,
strength of hands, and
will of hope.

NOTE FROM THE AUTHOR

Hello friend.

As you have witnessed, my passion, my purpose is positive poetry. It is a way to put good into our world. My hope is that you find this positive poetry inspiring, entertaining, and thought-provoking; that it gives you a bright spot in your day or maybe even helps you work through something difficult or spurs you on to have an adventure.

The gift of poetry is for me too. Writing poetry is the way I noodle-out things, plan, unplan, replan, notice, and find joy.

Please continue on this journey with me whether it is reading my positive poetry, attending one of my workshops, watching my YouTube channel, or taking advantage of my other offerings.

Visit me and write me at **www.createthedawn.com**.
We will create some sunrises and surprises together. -Dawn

Dawn Anderson

www.ingramcontent.com/pod-product-compliance
Lightning Source LLC
Chambersburg PA
CBHW070355110825
30913CB00009B/1034